1

MAKE PRAYER TIME AN APPOINTMENT.

- ❑ Two unforgettable disciples, Peter and John, kept their prayer appointment with God.

- ❑ Daniel prayed three times daily. The Psalmist prayed seven times daily. *Great men simply have great habits.*

- ❑ You make appointments with lawyers, doctors and friends. *Start making daily appointments with God.*

WISDOM FROM THE WORD

"Now Peter and John went up together into the temple at the hour of prayer, being the ninth hour."
Acts 3:1

DAY
2

ARM YOURSELF WITH SCRIPTURE.

- ❑ *God always remembers what He says.*
- ❑ He responds favorably to you when YOU remember what he says.
- ❑ When you approach God, He wants you to remind Him of His promises to you.

WISDOM FROM THE WORD

"If ye abide in me, and my words abide in you, ye shall ask what ye will, and it shall be done unto you."
John 15:7

DAY
3

DEVELOP DISCIPLINE.

❑ *The secret of your future is hidden in your daily routine.*

❑ Great achievers have success routines they follow diligently. They simply discipline themselves for a period of time *until a habit is born.*

❑ Develop a rhythm for your prayer life. It is the heartbeat of your spiritual life.

WISDOM FROM THE WORD

"As for me, I will call upon God; and the Lord shall save me. Evening, and morning, and at noon, will I pray, and cry aloud: and he shall hear my voice."
Psalms 55:16, 17

DAY
4

BELONG TO A PRAYER GROUP.

❑ Your private prayer life is powerful.

❑ However the Bible says that when two pray, something even more powerful takes place.

❑ Find a prayer group or birth a new group in your neighborhood or church. It could be the greatest contribution of your entire life.

WISDOM FROM THE WORD

"For where two or three are gathered together in my name, there am I in the midst of them."
Matthew 18:20

DAY
5

CHOOSE A PRAYER PARTNER.

❑ You cannot trust everyone with your private thoughts or problems.

❑ But, you need *someone*. One cannot multiply. Two is the secret to multiplication.

❑ Jesus introduced the Formula for Prayer Power. It's called the prayer of agreement. *Don't ignore it.*

WISDOM FROM THE WORD

"Again I say unto you, That if two of you shall agree on earth as touching any thing that they shall ask, it shall be done for them of my Father which is in heaven."
Matthew 18:19

DAY
6

DECIDE YOUR TRUE DESIRES.

❑ Few people really know what they want in life.

❑ *Name your needs.* Determine your burning desires.

❑ Now, speak them aloud to God. Boldly. *Expectantly.* Decisiveness is in your favor today.

WISDOM FROM THE WORD

"But without faith it is impossible to please him: for he that cometh to God must believe that he is, and that he is a rewarder of them that diligently seek him."
Hebrews 11:6

DAY
7

ELIMINATE DISTRACTIONS.

❏ *Atmosphere matters.* Protecting your focus is critical in releasing your faith.

❏ Separate yourself unto the Lord. Disconnect from outside influences.

❏ *Unclutter your hour of prayer.* Miracles are at stake.

WISDOM FROM THE WORD

"But thou, when thou prayest, enter into thy closet, and when thou hast shut thy door, pray to thy Father which is in secret; and thy Father which seeth in secret shall reward thee openly."
Matthew 6:6

DAY
8

USE SATAN AS A MEMO PAD.

❑ Every time you enter your prayer time, satan will remind you of something you forgot to do. It may be a telephone call to make or a letter to write, but it is designed to *break your focus.*

❑ *Keep a memo pad and pen handy as you pray.* When satan reminds you of something, simply write it down for later. Then say, "Thank you satan for being my memo pad."

❑ Now relax and enjoy your time with God.

WISDOM FROM THE WORD

"Lest Satan should get an advantage of us: for we are not ignorant of his devices."
II Corinthians 2:11

DAY
9

DON'T EDIT.

❑ *God already knows everything about you.*

❑ When you pray, be direct. Be honest. He rewards integrity.

❑ *Talk it out.* You can trust the One who made you. He's got all the time in the world. *Don't edit* your conversations with Him.

WISDOM FROM THE WORD

"And ye shall seek me, and find me, when ye shall search for me with all your heart."
Jeremiah 29:13

DAY
10

ENJOY HIS PRESENCE.

❑ *When you get into the presence of God, something happens that does not happen anywhere else.*

❑ Bring to Him your fears, worries, doubts and tears. You greatly matter to Him today. You really do.

❑ So, enjoy Him. He certainly enjoys you.

WISDOM FROM THE WORD

"Thou wilt shew me the path of life: in thy presence is fullness of joy; at thy right hand there are pleasures for evermore."
Psalms 16:11

DAY
11

EXPECT AN ANSWER.

❑ *Faith is confidence in God.*

❑ *Faith comes when God talks. It may be through a ministry, the Holy Spirit or His Word.*

❑ *Expectation is the invisible current that sweeps miracles into your life.*

WISDOM FROM THE WORD

"And it shall come to pass, that before they call, I will answer; and while they are yet speaking, I will hear."
Isaiah 65:24

DAY
12

EXPRESS YOURSELF FREELY.

❑ *Never be ashamed of your emotions.*

❑ God is emotional. You are made in His image.

❑ When you get into His presence, you can say anything you want ...any way you want to say it. He is simply thrilled you have come for a visit.

WISDOM FROM THE WORD

"And at the evening sacrifice I arose up from my heaviness; and having rent my garment and my mantle, I fell upon my knees, and spread out my hands unto the Lord my God."
Ezra 9:5

DAY
13

PICTURE YOUR MIRACLE.

☐ *God begins everything with a picture.*

☐ God pointed out the stars to Abraham to stir his faith for children. The woman diseased for 12 years saw a picture in her heart and it moved her to touch the robe of Jesus.

☐ Guard well the Miracle Picture God has placed within you. It is the *key* to your Miracle.

WISDOM FROM THE WORD

"For she said within herself, If I may but touch his garment, I shall be whole."
Matthew 9:21

DAY
14

PRAY YOUR EXPECTATIONS.

☐ *Words matter.* They create death or life.

☐ Your mind and your faith respond to anything you say.

☐ *Never verbalize anything you don't really want to happen.* Pray your expectations, not your experiences.

WISDOM FROM THE WORD

"For verily I say unto you, That whosoever shall say unto this mountain, Be thou removed, and be thou cast into the sea; and shall not doubt in his heart, but shall believe that those things which he saith shall come to pass; he shall have whatsoever he saith."
Mark 11:23

DAY
15

DON'T SABOTAGE A YESTERDAY PRAYER.

- ❑ Let's suppose you have just asked God for the salvation of your mate or loved one.

- ❑ He heard you. It mattered. He has promised a response.

- ❑ *Events are now in motion.* Don't come back today and speak words of doubt and unbelief to God or others. You may paralyze everything God is doing.

WISDOM FROM THE WORD

"But let him ask in faith, nothing wavering. For he that wavereth is like a wave of the sea driven with the wind and tossed."
James 1:6

DAY
16

ESTABLISH A PLACE FOR PRAYER.

- ❏ *Places matter to God.* He made them too, you know.

- ❏ Think of these places: The Upper Room, Jericho, Bethel, Zarapheth, Gethsemane.

- ❏ Jesus had special *places* for prayer. Mountains. Gethsemane. Go ahead...sanctify your own personal Prayer Place. It will become a precious and treasured Place.

WISDOM FROM THE WORD

"And when he had sent the multitudes away, he went up into a mountain apart to pray: and when the evening was come, he was there alone."
Matthew 14:23

DAY
17

PRAY IN THE NAME OF JESUS.

❑ Our Creator is interested in order.

❑ Remember, order is the accurate arrangement of things. *Approaching God requires spiritual protocol.*

❑ When you talk to the Father, come to Him... "In the name of Jesus."

WISDOM FROM THE WORD

"If ye shall ask any thing in my name, I will do it."
John 14:14

DAY
18

KEEP A
PRAYER LIST.

❏ Great intercessors often keep a map or globe of the world in their prayer room. They lay their hands on certain countries or cities as *a point-of-contact.*

❏ Others keep a *list of names* in the back of their Bible. It is a visual reminder.

❏ Since you are serious about effective praying, start your own Personal Prayer list today.

WISDOM FROM THE WORD

"I thank God, whom I serve from my forefathers with pure conscience, that without ceasing I have remembrance of thee in my prayers night and day."
II Timothy 1:3

DAY
19

LOOSE YOUR PRAYER LANGUAGE.

☐ French. German. Spanish. English. It is only natural that the Creator who thought of all the languages of the world...*has one of His own.*

☐ It is often called "a heavenly language." It is a personal and power-ful communication between a believer and his Father.

☐ Don't allow prejudice to rob you of this experience. *Explore its possibilities.*

WISDOM FROM THE WORD

"For he that speaketh in an unknown tongue speaketh not unto men, but unto God: for no man understandeth him; howbeit in the spirit he speaketh mysteries."
I Corinthians 14:2

DAY
20

LEARN SIX LEVELS OF THE LORD'S PRAYER.

❑ Jesus taught His disciples *how* to pray.

❑ There are six levels: 1) Praise 2) Priorities 3) Provisions 4) Pardon 5) Protection and 6) Praise, again.

❑ This little System for Prayer is quite powerful. Carefully and expectantly pray this prayer aloud today. *He taught it to us.*

WISDOM FROM THE WORD

"After this manner therefore pray ye: Our Father which art in heaven, Hallowed be thy name. Thy kingdom come. Thy will be done in earth, as it is in heaven. Give us this day our daily bread. And forgive us our debts, as we forgive our debtors. And lead us not into temptation, but deliver us from evil: For thine is the kingdom, and the power, and the glory, for ever. Amen." Matthew 6:9-13

DAY
21

FOCUS ON PRAISE.

❏ When Jesus taught His disciples how to pray, His first focus was on *entering the presence of God with praise.*

❏ He drew attention to the *Name of God.*

❏ So, today, begin praising God aloud for being Jehovah-Jirah (Provider), Jehovah-Shalom (Peace), Jehovah-Rophe (Healer), Jehovah-Nissi (Banner), Jehovah-Rohi (Shepherd), Jehovah-Tsidkenu (Righteousness).

WISDOM FROM THE WORD

"After this manner therefore pray ye: Our Father which art in heaven, Hallowed be thy name."
Matthew 6:9

DAY
22

FOCUS ON PRIORITIES.

❑ Let's pray this Prayer together:
"Father, I set myself in agreement
that the will of God shall be done
today...in my government...in my
church...on my job...and within my
home and family.

❑ You see my written list of things to
do. You know *the people* I am meeting
today. Remove those who do not
belong on my schedule. I speak to the
north, the south, east and west, and
call forth from the shadows of my
life those you have intended to be
linked with me.

❑ Father, *Your priorities* are mine.
Your will shall be done. I am led by
your peace, filled with your joy and
controlled by the Holy Spirit. In Jesus
Name, Amen."

WISDOM FROM THE WORD

"Thy kingdom come. Thy will be done in earth, as it is in heaven." Matthew 6:10

DAY
23

FOCUS ON PROVISIONS.

❑ Let's pray this Prayer together: "Heavenly Father, You are Jehovah-Jireh, my Provider. *Everything I have came from You.* Everything *in my future* will come from You. I don't have a thing You did not give me.

❑ Thank You for bringing the provisions I need for today. I trust You. My seed is in Your Hand. That is the proof I trust You.

❑ You are a Miracle God who provides supernaturally all the finances I need for today. It is done in Jesus Name, Amen."

WISDOM FROM THE WORD

"Give us this day our daily bread."
Matthew 6:11

DAY
24

FOCUS ON PARDON.

❑ Let's pray this Prayer together: "I thank you, Lord, for pardon, mercy and forgiveness. Thank you for forgiving me of my sins, my transgressions, my mistakes. Your peace and joy are filling me up as evidence that my record is spotless because of the righteousness of Jesus.

❑ Today, I forgive those who have sinned against me, hurt me and caused me harm in any way. I forgive them gladly because You showed mercy to me, and the servant is not above his Lord.

❑ I will walk in love, and forgive in advance anyone who may wrong me today. In Jesus' Name, Amen."

WISDOM FROM THE WORD

"And forgive us our debts, as we forgive our debtors."
Matthew 6:12

DAY
25

FOCUS ON PROTECTION.

- ❑ Let's pray this Prayer together: "Father, you will guide me away from temptation today and any trap planned by satan to destroy my life.

- ❑ You will deliver me from any strategy to harm me in any way. Thank you for Divine angelic protection.

- ❑ I have planted Seeds of faith that guarantee You will rebuke any devourer that rises up against my life. In Jesus' Name, Amen."

WISDOM FROM THE WORD

"And lead us not into temptation, but deliver us from evil: For thine is the kingdom, and the power, and the glory, for ever. Amen."
Matthew 6:13

DAY
26

FOCUS ON PRAISE AGAIN.

❑ Let's pray this Prayer together: "Father, I praise You again for influencing my *PRIORITIES* today... for *PROVISIONS*...for *PARDON* of every sin...for *PROTECTION* from every evil work.

❑ Now Your praise shall continually be in my mouth...You are my Healer, Deliverer, Savior and Miracle-Worker.

❑ I choose to trust You completely. You will not disappoint me. In Jesus' Name, Amen."

WISDOM FROM THE WORD

"And lead us not into temptation, but deliver us from evil: For thine is the kingdom, and the power, and the glory, for ever. Amen."
Matthew 6:13

DAY
27

STUDY THE CHAMPIONS OF PRAYER.

❏ *Heroes are worth observing.*

❏ The Bible is a Book of Champions. Read it carefully and you will see a parade of extraordinary people who changed the course of history *through their prayer life.*

❏ David, Daniel, Esther, Moses and Elijah are only part of the thousands of Champions...*Study their lives.*

WISDOM FROM THE WORD

"Elias was a man subject to like passions as we are, and he prayed earnestly that it might not rain: and it rained not on the earth by the space of three years and six months."
James 5:17

DAY
28

CONCLUDE TELEPHONE CONVERSATIONS WITH PRAYER.

❑ *Conversations are opportunities.*

❑ When you finish your telephone conversations today, simply say, "Let's have a brief word of prayer before I go."

❑ "Father, you've listened to what concerns us. We invite your influence and trust You for a miracle. Amen." *You have now provided God an Entry Point for a miracle.*

WISDOM FROM THE WORD

"Rejoice evermore.
Pray without ceasing."
I Thessalonians 5:16, 17

DAY
29

LET GOD DO HIS WORK.

❑ *Someone arrived here before you.* Your Creator.

❑ The composer has written his own song. *God has planned His own world.* Never forget it.

❑ *Get out of His way.* He is not a beginner. He will finish what He has started.

WISDOM FROM THE WORD

"The Lord will perfect that which concerneth me: thy mercy, O Lord, endureth for ever: forsake not the works of thine own hands."
Psalms 138:8

DAY
30

REPENT QUICKLY.

❑ Your mistakes and sins have not shocked God. He anticipated your need for mercy.

❑ *The Master Key to Recovery is Repentance.*

❑ Don't justify yourself. Quit blaming others for the decisions you have made. Repent. *Immediately.*

WISDOM FROM THE WORD

"He that covereth his sins shall not prosper: but whoso confesseth and forsaketh them shall have mercy."
Proverbs 28:13

DAY
31

SING ALOUD YOUR PRAYERS.

❑ Few have discovered this golden secret.

❑ Singing changes the climate and atmosphere...Stores even play it in the background during shopping hours. *There is a reason for it.*

❑ Do something different today. Sing out your prayer requests to God. You will be amazed at the joy and enthusiasm that rises within you.

WISDOM FROM THE WORD

"Let the Word of Christ dwell in you richly in all wisdom; teaching and admonishing one another in psalms and hymns and spiritual songs, singing with grace in your hearts to the Lord."
Colossians 3:16

"Speaking to yourselves in psalms and hymns and spiritual songs, singing and making melody in your heart to the Lord;" Ephesians 5:19

Decision Page

Will You Accept Jesus As Savior Of Your Life Today?

The Bible says, "That if thou shalt confess with thy mouth the Lord Jesus, and shall believe in thine heart that God hath raised Him from the dead, thou shalt be saved. For with the heart man believeth unto righteousness; and with the mouth confession is made unto salvation."(Rom. 10:9-10)

To receive Jesus Christ as Lord and Savior of your life, please pray this prayer from your heart today!

"Dear Jesus, I believe that you died for me and rose again on the third day. I confess I am a sinner. I need Your love and forgiveness. Come into my life, forgive my sins, and give me eternal life. I confess You now as my Lord. Thank You for my salvation, Your peace and joy. Amen."

Return This Today!

❏ Yes, Mike! I made a decision to accept Christ as my personal Savior today. Please send me my free gift copy of your book "31 Keys To A New Beginning" to help me with my new life in Christ. (B48)

"Sow A Seed Of Wisdom Into The Lives Of Those You Love!"

Here is your opportunity to invest in the lives of your Love Circle. Purchase 2 copies of *Seeds of Wisdom On Prayer* for only $5 for 2 special people in your life. These dynamic daily devotionals are your answer to the "Daily Bread" of the Wisdom of God.

❏ Yes, Mike, I want to Sow 2 *Seeds of Wisdom On Prayer* into 2 people that I love. I have enclosed $5 for the 2 books. Please rush them immediately. (SOW118)

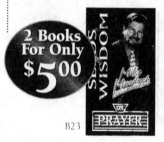

Send A Self-Addressed Envelope With Check Or Money Order To: Mike Murdock
P.O. Box 99 • Dallas, TX • 75221